THOUGHTS I CREATE OUGHT TO BE GREAT

BY KWAME JACKSON

Copyright © 2020 by Kwame Jackson

All rights reserved.

ISBN 978-1-7360707-2-7

First Edition

FOR KAYMAN AND KRUZ

I have the power
to choose and compare,
imagine potential,
and be self-aware.

I know my choices determine my fate, and everything great starts with mistakes.

As long as I learn

and improve what I do,

I will succeed

and know more than I knew.

I believe in myself,

and just like a seed,

belief determines

what I will be.

I know what's important

and know how to act.

I lead with love

to keep me on track.

I focus my thoughts

on things I desire.

I think and practice

like those I admire.

I treat people how
they want to be treated.
I look for root causes
and what's deeply needed.

I listen to friends.

They listen to me.

I understand first

and see what they see.

I make my goals

specific and clear.

I avoid danger

but don't live with fear.

I think about why

I do what I do.

If it feels good inside,

I see it through.

I know that habits

can be hard to break.

So I am careful

of habits I make.

I plan what I do

and do what I plan.

I change when I learn

and learn all I can.

I never quit,

and I never fail.

As long as I learn

and improve, I prevail.

If I feel pain,

I use it to grow.

I learn all the lessons

and then let it go.

The more that I live

the way that I plan,

the better I feel

about who I am.

I take the time

to quiet my mind,

and give thanks for all

that is good and kind.

www.ingramcontent.com/pod-product-compliance
Lightning Source LLC
Chambersburg PA
CBHW041704160426
43209CB00017B/1747